WHERE DO WE KEEP THE SCREWDRIVERS?

A SPOUSE'S GUIDE TO EMERGENCY PLANNING

BY LUCINDA HOFFMAN
WRITING AS LUCI HOFFMAN

 FriesenPress

One Printers Way
Altona, MB R0G 0B0
Canada

www.friesenpress.com

ISBN
978-1-03-919421-2 (Hardcover)
978-1-03-919420-5 (Paperback)
978-1-03-919422-9 (eBook)

1. REFERENCE, PERSONAL & PRACTICAL GUIDES

Distributed to the trade by The Ingram Book Company

Table of Contents

Introduction

Life can throw you curveballs in the form of an accident, an illness, a divorce, or even a death. This is not a guide to teach you how to grieve or how to manage the emotional trauma that comes with such an event. I am not a licensed grief counselor, pastor, financial advisor, or life coach. I am just an average retired, widowed woman who had to locate a lot of information in a brief period during an incredibly stressful situation.

On October 24, 2021, my husband passed away in his sleep. Since he had been ill for some time, we had the opportunity to "prepare" for this probable life-changing event. I soon found out that we could have prepared better and did not account for the emotional, mental, and physical stress that plays into the situation.

Since going through this experience, several of my friends have called me with questions regarding various aspects of this experience and how they might better prepare. I felt the importance of sharing the knowledge I gained so that others may benefit from my experience.

Purpose

The purpose of this guide is to help you take the initiative in gaining knowledge of and documenting that essential information that you may need to locate quickly and easily in the case of a family emergency. This guide is designed to help you more easily navigate the complex processes involved when a life-changing event occurs by helping you organize your information so that it is readily available.

It is not intended to steer you in any direction regarding budget, saving for retirement, or managing your portfolio. Those are decisions you must make on your own or with the help of a licensed and trained professional.

This guide is geared towards married couples. It is written from a woman's perspective because that is my life experience. I am sure, however, that it would also be helpful for non-married couples, parent/child relationships and even for those who are acting as legal guardians of other persons.

It would be especially helpful to have available for individuals who are acting as executors in the case of a death or who have power of attorney over another's affairs. If you are a single person, this information would be invaluable to your family if you should become disabled, incapacitated for any reason, or expire before having a chance to pass on this information to a loved one.

Part One

In Part One of this guide, I will share some real-life stories, experiences, and observations that may hit a nerve with some readers. The goal in Part One is to encourage the reader to be proactive when it comes to sharing and documenting knowledge about important family information.

The most common three stages that one goes through when experiencing a family emergency or death are also addressed. These are lessons born from my own personal experiences and are meant as a guide to assist you if, and when, you experience an emergency event of your own.

Chapter One: Life Lessons

A close friend of mine attempted for years to become more involved in the couple's shared finances, bookkeeping, taxes, and recordkeeping aspects of their household. Her spouse kept this information locked away in a room that she could not even get into to clean. This eventually led to her filing for a divorce. Luckily, through marriage counseling, her spouse was able to acknowledge and understand that she not only had a right to this information, but, as a spouse, it was her duty to be knowledgeable and be an active participant in the daily decision-making processes of their household. They found that working together towards common goals and sharing "knowledge" only made their relationship stronger.

It was a good thing he "saw the light" as not long after this, he fell off a two-story ladder and ended up incapacitated and in rehabilitation for a lengthy period, and she had to take over all "household" activities, including finances and taxes, and providing all required medical documents to hospitals and rehabilitation facilities.

There are many family dynamics that may come into play. Some families have one spouse who is typically the "handler" of the day-to-day operation of the home, finances, etc. The other spouse may be okay, or even thrilled, with this dynamic. Trust me, if you are not involved, or at least informed on a regular basis about what is happening with your finances, where important documents are stored, current password information, who to contact regarding different life occurrences, such as insurance, medical information, investment and tax details, and more, then "You are not doing yourself any favors!"

In some families, overseeing everyday affairs may become a struggle over power. I know many people who see knowledge as power. Again, addressing this issue is not my area of expertise; however, a heart-to-heart conversation with your spouse or loved one, explaining why you need to be "in the loop" may sometimes break the power barrier.

I give a big shout-out to those couples who consistently and equally share in the responsibility and record-keeping of the family affairs and information.

One of the key facts I learned during this entire process is that **everything you and your spouse own should be in both names."** That includes bank accounts, vehicles, boats, trailers, investment accounts, home, rental properties— EVERYTHING!!!! Otherwise, in the case of a death, probate court may be involved in determining what the surviving spouse is entitled to and delays in the transfer of property may occur.

I did not address any "business" information in this guide, such as LLCs, corporations, etc. If you own a business, contact your business attorney or tax consultant to see what information you should have readily available in case of an emergency. Please be aware that different states may have different rules regarding some legal applications regarding wills, trusts, etc.

Chapter Two: Stages of a Family Emergency

In my experience, there are three main stages to work through when dealing with a family emergency.

Stage One addresses items or processes that may require immediate attention within one to two weeks of the event.

Stage Two addresses items or processes that may require attention during the first month of a family emergency.

Stage Three addresses those items or processes that do not require immediate attention but will need to be resolved or addressed over the next few months.

These three stages are explained in more detail on the following pages.

Stage One

Stage one focuses on what needs to be acted upon immediately following the emergency.

If the family emergency involves a death, this stage may include dialing 911, dealing with a police officer, EMT personnel, a coroner, a hospital or nursing home, contacting a funeral home and pastor, and contacting family members and close friends.

Unfortunately, in today's world, some people make it a competition to be the first to post something on <Meta(Facebook)>. You do not want your family and close friends to find out about emergency situations or death on Facebook or any other media outlet before finding out about it from a family member.

This stage may also include arranging a funeral, with or without a pre-paid arranged funeral plan; writing an obituary; contacting someone to organize a funeral dinner; contacting the military or the American Legion for veteran acknowledgement; graveside services and funeral involvement; contacting newspapers; and handling a multitude of other details.

Luckily, I have four adult children, and their spouses, who were extremely helpful in these areas. I recommend asking someone, either a child, or children, or a close friend or relative, to assist you in this stage. Be selective. Too many cooks spoil the broth—if you know what I mean.

If the emergency is a result of an accident or a health emergency, then you may need to quickly provide health information such as insurance (Medicare and other); doctors' names and phone numbers; lists of current medications; income verification; and tax information. An attorney may become involved, and police reports and other information may be required.

Stage Two

Stage Two involves determining who needs to be contacted after the initial family emergency. This may involve enrolling your spouse in a long-term care or rehabilitation facility or scheduling health assistance to your home for a specific period. If a hospital or nursing home is involved, they may take care of the actual contacting of a rehabilitation facility but may still require information from you to make those contacts.

In the case of the death of a spouse, the second stage may involve contacting income providers for the deceased spouse. These providers may be the Social Security administration, employers, pension administrators, and other income sources. Health insurance and life insurance companies may need to be notified. More details on this are covered in the FINANCES section of this guide.

A death certificate will need to be provided and other information may be requested. Be prepared to spend hours on the phone. There may be long wait times and then you may be transferred to another person or given another phone number to contact, and the process starts all over again. Getting to the correct department and having the correct information in front of you does not always happen on the first call. Document all details of the discussions held on the phone calls and jot down contact names, phone numbers, fax numbers, and further instructions with each of these calls. When dealing with multiple companies, it may get confusing quickly. Who is sending you a packet? Who wants you to fax them information? Who wants a copy of the death certificate before any process may begin? Who wants you to send a copy of the death certificate in with the packet they send you to complete? Which pensions, if any, have a life insurance associated with it or a surviving spouse pension? Who needs an original death certificate vs. a copy of the death certificate? Chances are good that one phone call may not cover everything that needs to happen.

During one of my employment positions, I was the only female in a department of seventeen people. Several of the male employees liked to "sit and chat" each morning while drinking their morning coffee. I just wanted to get to work and had a tough time getting them to leave. One day I happened to sit my purse on the chair across from my desk. The first male co-worker came in, looked at my purse, and moved on. The second male co-worker came in, noticed my purse, thought about moving it, but moved on. I quickly realized that by placing my purse in that chair I had tapped into the childhood training where they learned "you never touch mama's purse!" From then on, I placed my purse in that chair when I wanted a productive morning.

In the case of a family emergency, it is okay to touch mama's purse or daddy's wallet. It may contain important documents such as insurance, driver's license, and Medicare information. There may be credit cards or important phone numbers stored in there. There may be reminders for appointments that you did not know about that need to be canceled or rescheduled. There may be gift cards and cash that need to go into a safe. You never know what you might find.

Stage Three

Stage three involves what needs to happen over the next few months. These are things that may not be as time sensitive as those listed in stages one and two.

This may include the following:

- changing the names on utility bills, insurance, automotive registrations, and properties,
- canceling debit and credit cards under the incapacitated or deceased spouse's name,
- changing the name and/or phone number on banking accounts and on checks,
- canceling gym memberships and other club memberships under the deceased's name.

In the case of death, incapacitation, or extended illness, you may want to consider canceling your spouse's phone. You may be able to keep the phone charged and still obtain contact information from it without paying for a phone plan.

Contact those persons who have your spouse as a main contact for maintenance purposes such as annual lawn mower, generator, propane tank fills, lawn service, etc. If these companies do not have a valid phone number to call, important maintenance may go undone.

Items in this stage will come to your attention over the next year in one way or another. You may receive an automatic deduction for a magazine subscription, gym membership, club dues notification, library book overdue fees, etc. Address these as they are received.

Part Two

Part Two outlines different categories of Information that you should consider documenting in preparation for a family emergency or death.

The categories include the areas of finances, sources of income, health, property, insurance, and commonsense.

There are worksheets available at the end of the book for each of these categories. Due to limitations on the size of the worksheets in this publication, you may want to consider downloading a free full-size (8.5" x 11") version from the website:

https://www.lucihoffmancreations.com

Chapter Three: Categories of Information

The information in this guide is grouped into five categories:

- finances,
- health,
- property,
- insurance, and
- common sense.

There is a checklist at the end of the guide for each category. A full-size version of this checklist is available for free on the website. Complete these worksheets with your spouse (or other "need to know" person). This checklist should be updated every time a password, account number, phone number, or any other valuable information changes. This happens more often than you may think.

I recommend using a pencil so that changes can be made more easily and keeping this information in a fireproof safe with your other important documents. Details on what you should keep in a safe are listed in the "Common Sense" section.

Chapter Four: Finances

Where is our money?

My husband used to ask me every Friday: "How are we doing on bills?" I would tell him the details but could see that he was zoning out about halfway through, somewhere between babysitter fees and groceries for the holidays. It finally got to the point where when he asked me, "How are we doing on bills?" I would reply, "Well, we had some money and now we don't." And he was okay with that answer.

Do you know your current financial status? Do you know where you keep your money? In the bank, or many banks? In investment accounts? In certificates of deposit? Do you know when any certificates of deposit come up for renewal? In an IRA? Cash in the safe or a lockbox? Points on a credit card or Sam's Club membership? Do you know who you owe money to? Do you have loans on vehicles, home equity lines of credit, personal loans, student loans, or credit cards?

All accounts should be in both names. In the event of a death, do not act too quickly to close a bank account. There are automatic deductions and deposits going into and out of that account that need to be addressed. My credit union did not make me change account numbers when my husband passed because we were both the owners of the account. That may not be true of all banks. If a will is involved, then an Estate account may need to be set up so that probate can track all income and expenses until such time that the requirements of the will have been met. In the State of Indiana, since everything was in both of our names, the will did not come into play.

Other things to consider: Who balances the checkbook? Consider taking turns doing this so you are both familiar with how it is done. Do you know where your spare checks are stored? Would you need to change the phone number on your checks if a phone was inactivated?

Chapter Five: Sources of Income

Where does your money come from? In the case of a death, the payer of the deceased must be notified immediately so that payments are stopped. Any payments made that are not valid will need to be fully reimbursed. If an automatic deposit was made through the bank, a reversal with the bank may be made. This may take several days. Social Security does not pay you in advance so if your spouse dies in October, for example, then he would be due the October payment because he survived part of that month. If a retirement benefit has been paid, you may receive a notice to pay it back, or, if there is a survivor benefit, they may deduct it from the survivor's future benefit.

When you contact the payer in the event of a death, they will provide you instructions to either fax information or wait for a packet in the mail. You may be required to send in their pre-approved form; a death certificate (some require originals, some will accept copies); a copy of your marriage certificate; legal divorce documents (if applicable); and some may require copies of social security cards.

If you are receiving a pension, you will need to know who is administering that pension. Many times, the company you worked for contracts with a bank, trust, or pension administrator to process your payments. Since pensions often change who manages their retirement payouts, I suggest you keep a copy of the latest Earning Statement in your safe. If you receive this online, make sure the website, username, and passwords are stored with your other important documents.

You will need to know when you, or your spouse, retired and the social security number of the payee. Are you receiving pensions from all eligible employers, or did you decide to wait until a later date to start some pensions? Do you know if your spouse elected a JOINT AND SURVIVOR option on their retirement?

What are your combined sources of income? Pensions, currently employed, social security, investment/IRA dividends, farm income, rental property income. Are you the main source of the income or a surviving spouse of the main source of the income?

COMPLETE THE FINANCIAL CHECKLIST AT END OF THIS GUIDE

You may download a full-sized version of the checklist in landscape mode for free from the website.

https://www.lucihoffmancreations.com

Chapter Six: Health

When my husband first became ill, we discussed what steps we needed to take to "get things in order." I highly recommend contacting an estate attorney to have a will, a Living Will, a Power of Attorney (in case you are in an accident or incapacitated where you cannot make decisions), and any other legal document(s) you and your attorney deem necessary for your individual situation such as a Living Trust, etc.

In addition, we had a current photograph taken of each of us and both of us together, paid for a plot in the cemetery, and prearranged our funerals so that we could each express our desires in that area. As a side note, my husband was a forty-one-year Veteran so we both qualified for a V.A. Funeral, which is less expensive than going to a funeral home. You still have all the options of a regular funeral. You just cannot have it in a funeral home. We chose to have ours at our church. It's worth looking into if you are a Veteran and haven't made any arrangements yet. I know this may sound morbid, but it is a reality. After being married for forty-five years we were comfortable with making these decisions together. It does not matter what your age is, these are decisions that must be made.

So, moving on. You should keep a current list of the medications that you and your spouse take, prescription and non-prescription. You should know where all the medications are kept—the ones in your daily dose containers and those being stored for future use, including those stored in the refrigerator. When my husband passed, the police had to take his medications with them, along with a list of his medications and his driver's license. Just a head's up.

You should know where the medications come from. What pharmacy, by mail, etc. If they are received through an online company like Express Scripts, you should know that website address, username, the account number, and password so that any future deliveries can be stopped. Otherwise, you may be paying for medications that may not be used.

Do you have access to medical and insurance cards? Do you have a list of your doctors and their phone numbers and physical locations? Do you have access to current medical records and medical history? These are things you may need to provide in case of emergency. If you have an online portal to your health information, do you know the website address and how to access it?

COMPLETE THE MEDICAL CHECKLIST AT END OF THIS GUIDE

You may download a full-sized version of the checklist in landscape mode for free from the website.

https://www.lucihoffmancreations.com

Chapter Seven: Property

What do you own? Is it in both of your names? This can be a broad category. We will begin with real estate property. Do you own a home? Is it in both of your names? Do you own a vacation property? Is it in both of your names? Do you own a rental property? Is it in both of your names? Do you own a farm? Is it in both of your names? You get the idea.

Knowing what you physically own is one thing. Knowing the details of those properties is quite another. Do you have a mortgage on your property? Who holds the mortgage? How much are the payments each month? If you paid it off, do you know where the deed is? Hopefully, it is in your safe, along with your other valuable documents.

Do you know what the personal property taxes are on your property? Do you know how much they are per year and when they are due and how you typically pay them? By check or by automatic deduction?

Regarding vehicles, do you know when the plates/registration are up for renewal? Do you have Roadside Assistance? Do you know who to call if either of you are involved in an accident? Do not depend on your spouse to provide this information. They may not be able to do so due to an illness or accident. This information should all be kept in your vehicle glove box.

COMPLETE THE PROPERTY CHECKLIST AT END OF THIS GUIDE

You may download a full-sized version of the checklist in landscape mode for free from the website.

https://www.lucihoffmancreations.com

Chapter Eight: Insurance

Home Insurance

Do you know who the insurance carrier is on your properties? Do you know the cost of your premiums each year? Do you know if you pay them annually, monthly, quarterly? Do you know who your insurance contact is? Do you know how it is paid? By check or automatic deduction?

Vehicle Insurance

Do you know who the insurance carrier is on your vehicles? Do you know the cost of your premiums each year? Do you know if you pay them annually, monthly, quarterly? Do you know who your insurance contact is? Do you know how it is paid? By check or automatic deduction? Do you know if you have a vehicle loan? Do you know if you opted to take the insurance that would pay the vehicle off in case of death? Check your loan agreement to see if you selected this option or waived it.

With whom do you insure your golf carts, boats, trailers, ATVs, or any other registered vehicle?

As a side note: If one of you becomes disabled for a period, you may be able to put one vehicle on "storage insurance" or at least have it reduced as you have two vehicles and only one driver.

Health Insurance

Do you know who your insurance carrier is? Do you have separate health insurance or are you covered under the same company? If covered under the same company, which one of you is it under? Do you know who it is paid to and how much it costs? Do you know who your insurance contact is? Do you know how it is paid? By check or automatic deduction?

If you are on Medicare or Medicaid, keep your annual statements in a safe place where they are easily accessible. These have important information in the case of reporting a death.

Accident Insurance

A few years ago, my brother and sister-in-law were in a serious ATV accident. They both suffered multiple life-threatening injuries and spent many months in hospital, rehabilitation, and recovery. They had opted for Accident Insurance coverage which paid for many of their monthly expenses such as home mortgage and car payments for several months. For them, it was a blessing.

Do either you, or your spouse, carry Accidental Insurance? If so, how much and with what company? Do you know the contact details for your Accidental insurance policies? Some banks and credit unions have a small accidental insurance policy associated with your bank account.

Life Insurance

Do either you or your spouse carry Life Insurance? If so, how much and with what company? Do you know the contact details for your life insurance policies?

COMPLETE THE INSURANCE CHECKLIST AT END OF THIS GUIDE

You may download a full-sized version of the checklist in landscape mode for free from the website.

https://www.lucihoffmancreations.com

Chapter Nine: Commonsense

I spent time with a friend teaching her how to use her sewing machine. She broke the needle straight away. She could not find the little screwdriver that came with the machine and spent twenty minutes in the garage looking for one. When her husband came home from the gym, he found one for her in the garage. That small job took thirty to forty minutes to complete. Do you know where your screwdrivers are?

This may be the most detailed section of this guide and may be the most important. It will cover a wide range of information. I am sure you can think of additional items to add to this list.

Contact Information

Can you readily find the names and phone numbers of those you should contact in case of a family emergency? Children, parents, siblings, close friends, pastor? Do you know the password on your spouse's phone in case you need to communicate with his/her closest friends regarding a family emergency? Is your spouse a Veteran? Do you know which Veteran organization(s) he is a member of? Do you know if your spouse is eligible for military honors as part of his/her funeral?

Memberships

Do you have memberships that need to be maintained? By maintained, I mean, do you pay for them? How do you pay for them? If these are deducted from your bank account automatically, you may need to cancel them.

Memberships may include gyms; the YMCA; the local zoo; American Legion and other private clubs; magazine subscriptions; the library; real estate and other associations; TV networks such as Dish, Direct TV, Hulu, Disney, cable, Amazon Prime, Microsoft Suite annual fees, etc.

Passwords

Passwords may change daily. Keep an updated list of passwords in your safe. Make updates in a timely manner. You may want to keep a copy in the safe of someone you trust as a back-up. Remember to provide them with an updated list on a regular basis, and I recommend putting a date on these lists, so you always know which ones are most current.

Cell Phones

Do you know who your cell phone plan carrier is? Do you know whose name the plan is under? Do you know the password on file for making authorized changes? Do you know your account number? Do you know how much your cell phones cost per month and how they are paid? By automatic deductions or by check?

What are your passwords for Google, Facebook, G-Mail, and your Voice Mail box? You need all of these if you change, or lose, your phone.

Internet Provider

Do you know who your internet provider is and how to contact them in case of loss of service or other service issues?

Utilities/Trash Pick Up

Do you know who provides your electrical, water, sewage, and trash pick-up services? Would you know how to contact them in case someone runs over or steals your trash can?

Lawn Maintenance

Do you know who does your lawn maintenance? This would include mowing, snow removal, shrub trimming, landscaping, fertilizing, weed control, bug control, rolling, etc. If it is your spouse, you are lucky. Who do you call for annual maintenance of your lawn mower and for power washing your house?

Tools

Where are the screwdrivers? The hammer? The tire pressure checker for when the tire is low. The pencil sharpener? Where are the jumper cables? If you find yourself asking your spouse where to locate certain items or documents on a continual basis, it is an indication that you may need to take a tour with him/her to see for yourself where items and documents are kept.

My husband had a challenging time finding certain items in the food pantry and refrigerator. The item could be right in front of his face, but he could not see it. He asked me over and over to consider alphabetizing the food pantry so he could more easily find things. Keep in mind that he never did any cooking, so I did not really see the point; however, to appease his need for organization I finally did it.

When he came in from mowing the yard, I told him I finally alphabetized the food pantry. His face lit up and he rushed over to see the results of my hard work. He turned to me with a confused look on his face. I explained to him that everything in a box was under "B" and canned goods were under "C." He never asked again. Many of you can appreciate this story but the point is, no matter how organized you think you are, the system you choose may not work for your spouse.

Keys

This is a big one. Where are the spare keys for your vehicles? Where is the key for the boat, the jet ski, and the snowmobile? Where are the keys for the lawn mower kept? Where are the keys to the outbuilding? Where are the keys to the three winding clocks and the two curio cabinets? Where are the keys to the whole house generator? What is the combination to the safe? Are there keys that belong to organizations that you may be involved with? Labeling the keys is very helpful. I have a whole drawer full of unidentified keys. I have no idea what they belong to but am hesitant to throw them away.

Alarms

Who are your alarm carriers? These could include burglar alarm systems, fire alarm and flood systems, doorbell alarm systems and cameras. If they are monitored, do you know the password if the alarm goes off and they call you? Do you know who to contact in case of maintenance emergencies? Some examples of emergencies could include dead batteries, loss of wireless internet, electrical issues, and damage from storms or animals. Do you know the passwords required to reset your wireless devices to communicate with your phone?

Pets

Do you know who your veterinarian is? Do you know when your pets are due for shots? Do you know where your pet's medical history is kept in case of emergency? Do you know where the cat carrier is?

Household Repairs

Do you know who to call for plumbing and electrical issues? Do you even know where the electrical panel is located? Do you know if you have a sump pump? A water filtration system? An in-floor heating system? Central air? Do you know where your equipment maintenance agreements are stored?

Chargers

This is a world full of rechargeable battery-operated equipment. To save yourself a headache, or three, I recommend labeling your chargers. I have two phone chargers for in the house, two phone chargers for in the vehicles, a tablet charger, a small car vacuum charger, two emergency light chargers, a drill charger, a screwdriver charger, chargers for two shrub trimmers, a mini chain saw, two nail guns, and several more tools in the garage. I do not even know what some of my chargers belong to. I just throw them in a drawer in case I figure it out some day.

Remote Controls

I highly recommend labeling your remote controls. I have three TVs in three different rooms, but the remotes all look alike. My grandkids are always moving them around, and I end up changing batteries that do not need changed because I am trying to turn on a TV with the wrong remote. However, this is just the tip of the iceberg.

We all have remotes for our televisions, electronic devices, air conditioners, window blinds, garage doors, ceiling fans, Christmas trees, recliners, stairway chairlifts. The list goes on and on. I have three remotes that I do not even know what they go to. I keep clicking them thinking something will happen, and then I can figure it out. I think one of them goes to a strand of Christmas lights I used to put on the plate rail in the kitchen at Christmas time. I may never find out.

Anyway, you get the idea. Labeling them with a permanent marker or a piece of tape is extremely helpful.

Tax Documents

Throughout the year you may accumulate tax information. Real estate taxes are usually paid in spring and fall and estimated Federal and State taxes are usually paid quarterly. Receipts for charitable contributions and deductible medical expenses may be collected all year long. Find a safe, easily accessible place to store these documents until tax time is here. It makes tax season less stressful.

The Safe

If you do not have a good fireproof safe, I would recommend buying one. You can get a decent sized one for around $600.00. There are some documents and items that cannot be easily replaced and some that cannot be replaced at all. It will be the best $600.00 you will spend. If you are robbed, you may lose that much, or more, in just your jewelry box contents.

I do not recommend keeping your passwords, user IDs, and account numbers in a document on your computer or stored in the cupboard next to your computer or anywhere in your house unless under lock and key.

I recommend that you memorize the combination to the safe or keep it in a safe location (no pun intended), and if it has an electronic keypad, know how to get into the safe if the battery runs out. When my mom passed away, she had provided the combination to my brother, but the battery had died. There is a special tool and method of getting a safe open in this situation. **Note:** Do not keep the instruction book to your safe in the safe!

I also recommend that you either provide the combination of the safe to one family member or tell them which drawer you have taped the combination under.

Here is a list of what I recommend you keep in the safe:
- guns and ammunition, and other weapons. (Do not ask.)
- passports,
- your birth certificates and those of your children,
- social security cards,
- death certificates,
- marriage certificates,
- legal divorce documents,
- cash, gift cards, rebates,
- valuable collections of any kind, such as coins and stamps,
- valuable jewelry,
- vehicle titles,
- deeds to any property you may own,
- loan documents that are unpaid,
- prepaid funeral arrangements,
- the checklists that you have prepared using this guide,
- a list of passwords,
- a list of current medications,

- a signed and dated list of who you want certain items to go to upon your death,
- a list of family heirlooms such as antique furniture, jewelry, and other items and who they originally belonged to in the family,
- special photographs such as wedding, graduation, etc. that you would hate to lose in case of fire (Be sure to identify who is in the photograph.),
- the location of any hidden cash you have in the house if you decide to hide it somewhere besides in the safe,
- copies of wills and other legal documents that have to do with trusts, powers of attorney, Living Wills, etc.

COMPLETE THE COMMONSENSE CHECKLIST AT END OF THIS GUIDE

You may download a full-sized version of the checklist in landscape mode for free from the website.

https://www.lucihoffmancreations.comv

I hope this guide has inspired you and your spouse, or other need-to-know person, to begin an initiative-taking approach in organizing your important data and safeguarding those items or information.

I encourage you to begin this process immediately and understand that gathering this information may take some time. Don't get discouraged. It will be worth it when completed, and you just might learn something along the way.

FINANCES WORKSHEET

Category could include banks, investments, individual retirement accounts, credit cards, debit cards, savings, certificates of deposit, checking, trust fund, mortgage loans, home equity lines of credit, personal loans, and auto loans.

CATEGORY	TYPE OF ACCOUNT	NAME OF BANK OR COMPANY	ACCT NUMBER	PIN #	CONTACT & PHONE

SOURCES OF INCOME WORKSHEET

Sample sources of Income could include current employment, retirement, social security, investments, IRA distributions, rental property income, farm income, sale of a business, etc.

SOURCE OF INCOME	WHOSE INCOME?	NAME OF SOURCE	ACCT NUMBER	PIN #	CONTACT & PHONE

MEDICAL CHECKLIST

DR. OR INSURANCE CO.	TYPE OF DR. OR INSURANCE	WHOSE DR?	WEBSITE/ACCT #	PIN # OR PW	CONTACT & PHONE

PROPERTY CHECKLIST

Type of property could include home, rental, vacation, auto, truck, boat, camper, or trailer.

TYPE OF PROPERTY	ADDRESS OF PROPERTY	LOAN ON PROPERTY?	LOAN WITH WHOM?	ACCT #	CONTACT & PHONE

INSURANCE CHECKLIST

Type of insurance could include home, rental, auto, life, boat, camper, trailer, atv, accident, etc.

TYPE OF INSURANCE	CARRIER	POLICY NUMBER	CONTACT & PHONE

COMMONSENSE WORKSHEET

This worksheet may contain a variety of information. There are no titles at the top of the worksheet columns so you may add your own. Some of this information may include contact information, memberships, passwords, cell phones, internet, utilities companies, lawn maintenance, tools, keys, alarms, pets, household repairs, chargers, remote controls, tax documents, and safe contents.